# Contents

# ACKNOWLEDGMENTS

I give thanks to my heavenly Father who chose me, even when I was not sure I was ready to be chosen. To my husband, thank you for understanding when my school studies caused me to neglect some things around the house. Thank you for making sure I ate on those nights I was writing yet another paper. Thank you for believing in me always. To those family and friends who support me unconditionally you know who you are, and thank you for the love. Words cannot express how excited I am at this time to finally have my book in print. I want to say a special thanks to Pastor Kisia Coleman. You are a trailblazer who often leads the way for others to follow. I have been so encouraged by all of the things you do and are accomplishing with your ministry. From our very first meeting at your Women's conference, I have looked forward to what you were going to do next. Your book "The DO IT Mandate" was just what I needed to get "I'm Doing It! Finished.

## The Beginning

This book came into existence after many years of me saying that I was going to write a book. My exact words were "I should write a book," "I wanna write a book" "I'm going to write a book one day" "Is she can write a book, I know I can write a book." I have actually been writing for years. First, I wrote in my diaries, then I wrote teen girl fiction, next I wrote adult woman fiction and poems. The poems usually came about when I was going through a rough time in my life. Man problems, friend problems, children problems or money problems.

I have had a very strong urge to write since I was in sixth grade. When I would get an urge to write, my mind would become full of thoughts that I had to get on paper. I used to stay in my room, content to read and write. Sometimes I didn't wan to go outside to play. I was happy with my thoughts and a new table and pen.

One day my mom made me go outside to get sone air. I remember standing outside the front door kicking it and crying because I wanted to go back inside to read and write. When I moved down south to go to high school, I did not go to the neighborhood recreation center like most of the other young people. I stayed at home writing.

Years ago, my mother asked me if I was every going to try to get anything published. At that time, I had never thought about getting my work published, and just the thought of someone reading my words horrified me. My writing was just for me. Storylines and adventures from deep inside my imagination filled sheets and sheets of paper. All of this was for my eyes only so, it was a great surprise to me this year when the urge to write for publication became to strong that I knew the time had come for me to share my thoughts with others. I chose the book title for several reasons.

**"I'm Doing It!"** is a declaration for all of the years I have put things off. I am a procrastinator. "My name is Conchetta Jones, and I am a procrastinator" I know that some of you who know me may be saying, "yes, you sure are" Others may be a little surprised. Recently a close friend of mine was surprised when I told her I was a procrastinator. She said, "I never would have believed that of you. You always seem so on task, with your "to do" lists." Sometimes I wait until the last minute to do things. Right mom? My mother's birthday is August 13. I have not mailed off her birthday card at this writing. (Oct. 3) and usually end up taking it down south with me when I go down for Thanksgiving or Christmas.

I always have really good reasons for waiting to do things. I am sure a lot of you reading this are the same way. Here are a few of my reasons for waiting. See if you recognize yourself in any.

- I waited until I had more education
- I waited until the time was right
- I waited until my son was old enough
- I waited until I had a job
- I waited until I had a better job
- I waited until I had another's approval

- I waited until someone else did it first

- I waited until I had lost/gained some weight

Sometimes I didn't do things I knew I was called to do because I was afraid I did not know enough. If I was not 100% sure of how to do something, I would not attempt it. I felt I needed to study on the topic until felt comfortable with it. This often took too much time and the opportunity was missed. Sometimes I was afraid of what others thought our would say.

Now don't get me wrong, this did not apply to all areas of my life. I am naturally an independent, confident person. My sisters might say bossy. As long as I was doing something I wanted to do, enjoyed doing it, and felt it was within my comfort zone, then I was good to go. When it came to modeling, or anything fashion related, I was ready I never procrastinated. My "model" bag was always packed and I was always ready for the next fashion show. I was not afraid to walk across that stage; the more people watching the better.

When it came to public speaking, I was scared stiff. I put off taking Communications 103 because I had to speak in front of the class. The whole class was writing and making speeches. I failed this class two times, at two different colleges, in two different states because I could not stand in front of the class to deliver my speeches. Just standing in front of a room talking was very scary to me. Fear will immobilize you. It will stop you from accomplishing the things you want or need to do.

Over the years God has been trying to bring me out of my comfort zone. He was ready for me to stop doing my thing and start doing his thing. He has been ready and waiting for me to act for some time now. But His thing scared me. For it would definitely take me out of my comfort zone. For starters He made me the wife of a preacher. Not just a preacher, but a Pastor.

Really God? During that time, I had been out of church for years and spend a lot of time in the nightclubs. So, I procrastinated. I had to be sure. I had to be really sure that God was calling me to be a minister's wife. I was having way too much fun partying. I questioned God. I said I needed to be crystal clear. I wanted a sign. God made it crystal clear to me that yes you are to be a preacher's wife. Be careful when you ask God for proof, it can be a bit much to experience. Take my word for it.

The first few years I was out of my comfort zone. There were a lot of expectations for me. Some came from external. There were external expectations, like people just expecting me to speak because I was the First Lady of the church. I don't know how many times I have had to remind people that my husband is the anointed one, not me. Just because he speaks, don't expect me to.

Some expectations were internal. I put them all on myself. But as I found out, when God calls you to do a thing, He is also right there to prepare you. He is taking each step. Leading and guiding your path. If needed then He carries you until you get your footing. That is why I love the poem **"Footprints"** It has special meaning to me because there have been many times He has had to carry me.

When I stopped ignoring God's quiet voice and started stepping out in faith, things started to happen. Some were big faith things. Like the time I was asked to be a Women's Day speaker. Lady Sharon Lindsey actually told my husband she was going to ask me to speak. My husband knew how I felt about speaking in church, but he told her to go ahead and ask me. I think he was surprised when I accepted.

I think God has a great sense of humor. I had just made up my mind that I was not going to tell the Lord no ever again. I felt that if somebody thought I had something to say, then say it I would. By then I had mustered up the courage to start speaking more at my own church where I am known and loved.

I had been thinking about doing little things like being Mistress of Ceremony at our programs or leading the devotion during our services. I truly was not thinking about speaking in front of a church filled with people, some of them ministers. I thought I was going to run from the place that Sunday afternoon when my husband and Pastor Lindsey took seats right in front of the pulpit, and they showed me to the Pastor's chair. A big imposing leather one. Really God? Really?

The second big thing happened about four or five months later. I was asked to be one of several speakers at a women's retreat. I was the only speaker that was not a minister. When I remind people that I am not a minister, they remind me that I still have a message to share.

I was the fourth speaker of the morning. The first three were fiery speakers. They were dynamic and had the room rocking. Women were shouting amen and standing on their fee. For those of you who knew Dr. Armitta Epps, you know that she was powerful. She was the speaker who spoke before me. I told you about God and his humor right? Dr. Epps was a great friend of my husband and I. We were often attending services at her church. She was power with a capital "P"

Women were up on their feet, praising the Lord. There was a fire in the room. I sat in my chair thinking about how I could leave the building without telling anybody. I didn't think anybody would miss me. I had sat all morning going over my notes and changing things. I no longer felt that my little message was good enough. The little confidence I had when I arrived was already gone. I was ready to cry.

The lady who had invited me to be one of the speakers must have noticed my face. She came up to me and asked me if I wanted prayer. "Yes please" I whispered. She had me follow her to a small room, where several other women waited. They circled me and started praying. I could feel the strength returning to me.

When it was my turn to face the women and speak, I felt like my knees were knocking so loud everyone in the room could hear them. After a quick prayer, I gave my prepared message. It was surprising to me, that it was very well received. The women in the room were nodding in agreement and as I took my seat women reached out to hug me or nod encouragingly. I will always be grateful to a woman who attended the retreat. I saw her several months after the retreat and she told me that my message had stuck with her. She even quoted to me some of the things I had said that Saturday morning.

Some of the other things that happened to me when I stopped ignoring God's voice were small. It became easier for me to get up in front of the members at my church to speak. I even spoke for our Women's Day service. All of this was enough for me to know that God was working in my life, in a mighty way. It explains all of the unhappy times I had to endure. It explains all of the people that came into my life, some for a season, all for a reason.

For those who hurt me I say thank you. Every time you did me wrong it sent me running to God and made my relationship with Him closer and stronger. It made my relationship with him solid. When I had no one else to turn to, I knew I could always call on Him. For those of you who have always had my back I say thank you. Your love and support have made me the strong woman I am today.

**SOMETHING TO THINK ABOUT:**

In what area of your life is God carrying you until you get your footing?

# Friends

Sometimes the people you hang with can stop you from **doing it.** Yes, your friends can hold you back! Yes, those friends who you think of as family can stop you from moving on up! You should surround yourself with people who are positive. If you are always around negative people you soon begin to think like them. You begin to only see the bad in any situation. Your cup starts to always be half empty instead of half full. The world begins to be a big, scary place for you.

Negative people are only happy when they are bashing someone or something. Have you ever noticed that you can be having a lovely day and a negative person come around and suddenly the atmosphere changes? They always find something wrong. It the sun is shining they will complain that it is too hot, too bright, not high enough, not hot enough. They are never satisfied and can always find the worst in everything and everybody.

You must be very careful about who you have around you. The people in your life need to be doing something. They should have goals. They should be positive about what is going on in their life and also in yours. They are the motivators who push you when you are hesitant to step out there. They want the best for you. They want to see you succeed. They rejoice with you when you are winning.

Be wary of the friend who is positive about their life, but not yours. If you are around someone who always has to be the center of the conversation, watch out. If they are always ready to discuss their problems, or their triumphs, but never seem to have the time or interest to talk about yours, then that is a problem. If it always has to be about them, then you might want to take a second look at that relationships.

You also need to know that if you are the smartest person in your circle all of the time, then something is wrong with your circle. You need to have someone that knows more than you about some things. You need to have someone to look up to. You need room to grow. You need people who are where you want to be. The old saying iron sharpens iron is right on. You need to be able to aspire higher. You should want to soar.

Pigeons do not soar with eagles. There are some people who are content to stay where they are, doing the same old thing. Don't settle.  There are also people who like the fact that they are the person with all of the answers. They like always being the one in the group that everybody looks up to. It makes them feel important when others have to come to them for advice. ALL OF THE TIME!

Don't desire to be that person. It is not a good thing, no matter how good it makes you feel. It means you will stop growing. You will become stagnant. We are forever evolving. Never be content or satisfied when you have reached a goal. Set another one.

You should always be willing to learn something new. I am a life-long learner. I love being a student, whether in the classroom or of life. I want to learn new things. I get excited when I read a book or attend a workshop. I love being around smart people too. Lately I have had the opportunity to be around some brilliant people. I am open to all of the information they are willing to share. I don't have a problem asking for information. I think it is so silly when people refuse to use their resources. (That is part of the Girl Scout Law) Use resources wisely. It must be a pride thing, but I love it when people succeed. Because if God has done it for them, then I know He can do it for me too.

You will notice that when you start doing a new thing that some people will not like the change. They may start to make catty, snide remarks. They may even stop wanting to hang around with you. They may stop taking your calls. Don't despair. Those are the people who don't need to be in your inner circle anyway. Remember the season or reason people? Even Jesus had His inner circle with His select few. Everyone is not going to be able to soar with you.

Some people are there for a reason or a season, and their season just may be up! Don't try to hold on. Doing so will only hold you back and stop you from doing what you are called to do. I had this type of friendship once. We were both in bad places in our lives and we used to have pity parties together. If I needed someone to complain with, I knew she would be there. We would call each other early morning and late night. So, you can imagine how our lives were.

We started our days off with our negative outlooks early in the mornings and ended our evenings with more of the same. Cindy Trimm says we should command our mornings. We need to be very careful what we are thinking about and make sure our words are positive. We should make it a habit to examine what our thoughts are chasing after and what our words are gathering to us. A negative outlook in the morning can poison the whole day. Needless to say, neither one of us accomplished much during our one year as close friends.

If you have a friend or friends who make jokes, makes you feel silly when you tell them about a plan or goal or dream of yours, then let that person go. Immediately! And don't feel bad about it, even if it is a family member or members. You need some movers and shakers in your life. Those are the people you want to get to know and want to rub shoulders with. The longer you hang around with people who laugh at you or make fun of you, the longer you will put off **doing it. Remember doing it is your goal.**

## SOMETHING TO THINK ABOUT:

Who are the pigeons in your life?

Who are the family members or friends who laugh at you and make you feel silly when you tell them your plans to soar?

Who are the eagles you need to spend more time with?

# Procrastination

Procrastination is the act or habit of procrastinating, or putting off or delaying, especially something requiring immediate attention. That is the definition from the dictionary. Procrastination is another reason we don't get anything done. It was one of my biggest problems. I would always put things off until the next day, which became the next week, month, year. You see where I am going with this right?

God gave me ideas of businesses to start, classes to take, people to contact, books to write, and I kept putting it off for a better time; the right time. I was waiting for the right amount of education to write that book, go after that job. Year after year I would push the idea away until a later time or a better time.

Procrastination doesn't pay. When I finally decided to act, to do whatever it was that I had put off, it was too late. The opportunity for me was gone. Someone else had taken the idea and run with it. So where it would have been an open playing field for me, by the time I got around to doing it, there was a lot of competition. The market was saturated. Ecclesiates 3:1 says that to everything there is a season, and a time to every purpose under the heaven. There is a time for everything. It is your time when the urge is there.

Procrastinating didn't mean that I couldn't do it, it just meant my edge was gone. I would be one in a sea of many. I would have to work harder. Waiting can cause you to miss your season of grace. I would often say things like "I work better under pressure" I think I really believed that but, it wasn't true. The stress that I put myself under was not good. The nights that I stayed up finishing a paper because I had put it off was frustrating and stressful. The fact that writing comes easy to me is not a good excuse. I could have used the extra sleep. And life happens.

Once I had computer problems and spent a few anxious hours because my paper was due the next day, it was late night and my computer was doing its thing. It was frozen and for like an hour nothing was happening. I was so afraid I had lost my work. I didn't, but it would have been so much better if I had not waited until the final hour huh?

I always feel bad when I put off doing things. Procrastinators often tell themselves that everything is under control. That they can wait a little longer. Procrastinating is a main tool of the enemy. So go from planning to do, to doing.

**Famous Quotes**

"Never put off till tomorrow what may be done today" – Mark Twain

"Only put off until tomorrow what you are willing to die having left undone" – Pablo Picasso

"You may delay, but time will not" – Benjamin Franklin

"A day can really slip by when you're deliberately avoiding what you're supposed to do" – Bill Watterson, Calvin and Hobbs

"Let's take care of the little things while they're still little" – John G. Miller

"To procrastinate obedience is to disobey God" – Randy Alcorn

"Procrastination is the foundation of all disasters" – Pandora Poikilos

"Procrastination is opportunity's natural assassin" – Victor Kiam

**SOMETHING TO THINK ABOUT:**

In what areas of your life do you have the biggest problem with procrastination?

# Fear

Fear is another reason we put off **doing it!** Whatever "it" is. We are afraid we will fail. We are afraid people will laugh at us, talk about us, judge us. We should never let fear stop us from acting. God has not given us the spirit of fear. (2 Timothy 1:7) There is no place for fear in our lives.

Fear is a killer. It is a killer of dreams. Fear will keep you from making moves. It will keep you in one place; a place where you feel safe. When you are afraid you breathe quicker and your heart beats faster. You think of all of the bad or negative things that could take place. Sometimes our fears are unwarranted.

Once some years ago I was getting into my car on a very windy Chicago day. I had just put my grocery in the trunk and back seat and my hair was blowing all around my face. It got in my face as I got into the front seat. After I closed the door and went to start the car, I found I couldn't move. Something was pulling me by my hair. My hear started beating quicker and I couldn't move. So you can imagine how I felt when I did muster the nerve to turn around and saw that I had closed my hair in the car door. I immediately started to laugh. I had been so frightened for nothing. That is how it is when we let fear stop us from doing the things we want to do. We become paralyzed and we don't move.

When there is something that we know we should be doing and, we are not doing it because of fear, then we are going to have to do it afraid. Joyce Meyer has a book **Do It! Afraid**. In it she talks about how we should not let fear stop us from following our destiny. Being afraid should not stop you from acting. It should not paralyze you. It means that you are going to go ahead and do it afraid for a little while.

In the Bible there were some people who did it afraid. Moses was not too eager to speak to Pharoah. He came up with all kind of excuses. Esther was a Queen who risked her life for her people. When she tried to resist her cousin's request that she intervene with the King on their behalf he asked her. "Who knows but that you have come to royal position for such a time as this?" Are you in a particular position because there is something that you should be doing?

You might feel that you have waited too long and you are too old. Well, do it old. Abraham and Sarah were old when they had their son Issac.

On the other hand, you might feel that you are too young at this time. Then do it young! King David, Joseph, Mary and Jesus were a few of the people in the Bible who did it young. No matter what limitations you feel are keeping you from doing the things you are called to do or want to do, **Just Do It!**

I was afraid to act because I was too busy thinking about the "what ifs" What if I did something and it did not come out as I had planned. What if I said the wrong thing at church? Remember fear will immobilize you. It will stop you from accomplishing the things you want to do. What if people talk about me? What I found out is that people will talk about you anyway. So that should not be a stopping point or deal breaker for you. Whether you are doing something or not doing anything, some people will still have something negative to say. The best way to shut a hater's mouth is to succeed. Then if they still talk, now you have given them something to talk about.

Take a chance. Step out of there. If there is something you want to do, if you have great ideas, but have been waiting to get started, if you have an urge, a yearning or desire to do…then **Do It!**

**Famous Quotes**

"Do one thing daily that scares you" – Eleanor Roosevelt

"Our deepest fear is not that we're inadequate. Our deepest fear is that we are powerful beyond measure" – Marianne Williamson

"There is only one thing that makes a dream impossible to achieve; the fear of failure – Paulo Coelho

"Expose yourself to your deepest fear, after that, fear has no power, and the fear of freedom shrinks and vanishes. You are free" – Jim Morrison

"fear of name increases fear of the thing itself" – J.K. Rowling

"Don't give in to your fears. If you do you won't be able to talk to your heart" Paulo Coelho

"The only thing we have to fear is fear itself" – Franklin Roosevelt

**SOMETHING TO THINK ABOUT:**

What is it you have been wanting to do, but have been afraid to do?

# Roadblocks/Hindrances/Obstacles

A roadblock is an obstruction used to halt traffic. A hindrance causes delay. An obstacle is a thing that blocks one's way or prevents or hinders progress. Do you have any of the above in your life and they are stopping you from doing anything? Some roadblocks to keep you from **"doing it"** are the words you use and the thoughts you think.

How many times have you said? "I'm going to" When are you going to? If you think back to all of the times you used that phrase what was the ending to the sentence? What were you going to do? Did you ever do it?

For me some of the endings were…"I'm going to…write a book" "I'm going…back to school" "I'm going to…start a business" "I'm going to…learn how to swim" These were just a few. It took me until 2001 to make going back to school a reality. And I wonder if I would have gone back then if the job that I had at the time had not required it.

When you get stuck in the "I'm going to" mode then it's hard to get out. Life happens, things come that will take you mind off of what you were going to do. And sometimes the things that come seem so important that you don't see them as roadblocks, hindrances or obstacles.

How often have you thought, that of course you should put your dream aside and babysit your grandchildren while your daughter/son does their thing. After all it's your grandchildren. They didn't ask to be here. It's not their fault that their parents are irresponsible and lazy. How often have you thought it's the right thing to do to put off your doctor's appointments because you need to do something for someone else. These things sound noble and many women put themselves last while they put everyone else's needs first.

When you push your needs and wants way down on the list it is not good. Sometimes you have to put yourself first so that you are able to take care of others. If you have every flown, you know that during the flight attendant's safety speech she tells you that in the case of an emergency and oxygen is needed you should place the mask over your face first, and then over the infant/child who is traveling with you.

It makes common sense. If you pass out the baby can't help you. I once heard a woman declare "I couldn't do that my baby comes first" I just shook my head. Her thinking was all wrong. And because I personally know her, so is her life. Her priorities are way off course and she often wonders why things don't seem to ever work out for her.

Are you the mother who will work two jobs so your children can have the latest gadgets and name brand clothes? Are you the woman who works and takes care of all of the bills while your guy stays at home playing video games? He won't watch the children or life a finger to help around the house. He even has the nerve to criticize the things you do. (more on that later)

How often have you said "I'm going to stop buying $200 gym shoes or  $100 jeans for my teenage son/daughter" or "I'm going to put his lazy butt out" "I'm going to" can be some very powerful words, which often are just that, words, because we usually do nothing.

Negative thoughts and speech create circumstances. They prevent us from doing the things we need or want to do. Negative thoughts are those little voices in your head telling you that you can't do something. When you find that happening you have to stop it immediately.

We have to be careful what we think about. Sometimes those negative thoughts appear in our minds just out of the blue. When we let them stay, we begin to dwell on them. We soon believe those words and soon we are saying we can't do something.

These are some words that we need to remove from our vocabulary. They are negative and when we say them enough, they take on a life of their own. They prevent us from doing the things we need or want to do. Words are powerful. There are three words that I want to talk about: "can't" "but" and "try"

When you use the word "can't" you put things in the realm of impossibility. You are opening the door to you not being able to do it, and since you think you can't, you won't. One of my experiences with using the word can't is what I call my Jiffy cornbread story.

Years ago I made a bad pan of Jiffy cornbread. For some reason it did not rise and it was hard. I don't know what I did wrong this particular day, but after that incident I started saying "I just can't make Jiffy cornbread. I would say it in a joking manner. I had been making cornbread since I was a little girl. I still remember making my first pan of cornbread. I was in first or second grade. We still lived in Meridian. I wonder if my mom remembers that evening. I had my own little pan of golden brown cornbread. But my Jiffy experiences started out being hit or miss, and I continued saying I couldn't make it.

As the time passed and I continued saying it, my Jiffy cornbread got worse and worse. I know what you are thinking. "Really? Jiffy cornbread? There is nothing to it" And I agree with you, but since I have put those words out there, I have not been successful in making a fluffy, golden brown pan of Jiffy cornbread. That is going to change because my words have changed. I have stopped saying that I can't make Jiffy cornbread.

Intimidation is another roadblock. We can become so intimidated by others that we presume to be better off than we are. Instead of getting to know them better and learning all we can from them, some of us will stay away. We see them as larger than life. We are so blinded by their accomplishments that we can't imagine doing the same or more. I call that having the grasshopper mentality.

In the Bible in the book of Numbers, Moses sent men to spy out the land of Canaan. He wanted them to find out what was going on in the land. After searching, the spies found out that the land had grapes so big that it took two men to carry a branch with one cluster on it.

The land was also flowing with milk and honey. The people living in the land at the time were strong. They were the children of A-nak. These were men of great stature and considered to be giants. Two of the spies felt confident enough to go and take the land. But, ten of the spies gave the report that they would not be able to go against the people for they were stronger than them. They said that in their own sight they were as grasshoppers.

Out of their own mouths they claimed to be grasshoppers. Now we know that a grasshopper is a very tiny creature. Feeling that way will certainly stop you from doing anything. Aren't you tired of being a grasshopper?

Now let's go back to our circle of friends. That is another hindrance we need to watch out for. That would be those people who are content with their circumstances. They are still doing the same thing at 30, 40, 50 and older that they were doing in their early 20's. Nothing is sadder that seeing someone dressing, acting and reacting too young.

Years ago, when I used to party, I was at the Cotton Club on Michigan Avenue in Chicago. The club was set up so that there was mellow jazz playing up front and loud dance music playing in the back.

This particular night an older gentleman made his way to the back. I watched as he tried to pick up several young women. They were young enough to be his granddaughters. He looked so out of place, almost pathetic. And when he asked a whole table of women "What's going on foxes?" they burst out laughing.

He asked me to dance and I said yes. I was a dancing machine back then. I danced that old gent for about 30 minutes straight. House music was playing and it just kept going and going and going. I would not make eye contact with him as we danced. I knew he was getting tired, but I didn't care.

He finally got my attention and huffed that he needed to get back to the front. This is just a reminder that you need to stay in your lane. Your child does not really want to see you getting your groove on at the club.

Okay, so to continue talking about our friends. There is the friend who does not want to do anything to better herself or himself and is upset when you do. We all have that friend who is content in that low paying job or getting her Link card and selling part of it each month.

Now don't get me wrong. Public Assistance is there for those who need it, and that is not what I mean at all. I mean those that abuse the system. They are not even trying to look for a job or go to school, or do anything else to better themselves. They are content to collect public assistance year after year. They raise their daughters to collect public assistance.

It becomes a generational thing. The children soon believe that it is the only route to take. We are children of the King. We do not have to settle for a meager handout from the government.

Our small thoughts produce small results. Cindy Trimm says that if our thoughts are inferior then our life will also be inferior. Sometimes we continue to hang with the same friend we've hung with for years even though it no longer fits. It is because we've known them since we were children. They are like family. You know it's not good, because whenever you tell them your hopes and dreams they laugh at you and spew out some negative comments on why you won't succeed.

They make you feel silly for even thinking you could succeed ad so you push your dreams back down. You take their word because after all they know you so well. If they say it won't work then it probably won't. Now is the time to pull your dreams up and out. It is your time. You may have to leave some people when you decide that it is time to **"do it"** Whatever "it" is.

Family members often hinder us. We have those family members who always make their problems our problems. They have bills they can't pay, they need a babysitter, a ride, bus fare, a loan until payday, to spend a few nights on your couch. Whenever they call you, the first thing out of their mouth is "Girl/Man I need a favor"

We feel obligated because after all it is my sister, brother, cousin, etc. You push aside your plans to help out a family member. And even though you feel disappointed you believe that you are doing the right thing. You feel righteous and Christian like.

It doesn't matter that most of the time these family members are in a bad place because of their lack of responsibility. They chose to play hard while you choose to work hard. I saw an episode on the *Judge Mathis* show where a young man felt because his brother and sister-in-law had won the lottery, he was entitled to some. He felt their good fortune was his time to come up (benefit from their good fortune)

How many of you have those kind of family members? They count your money for you. You actually have the nerve to feel bad for them. Really?

Don't feel obligated to help them. We are all given the same seven days, 24 hours a day. It is how we choose to use that time that matters. As I have stated there are those who genuinely need our help, and we should be that help. We all need help at some time or another. God blesses us to be a blessing to others. But don't fall into the trap of being used or made to feel guilty because of God's favor in your life.

Don't continue to give, give, give. Don't continue to be used just because it is a family member. If you re crowned with favor…walk in it.

Don't keep thinking, "It's my family, it's all good, right? "That's what family is for, right?" Not so much. There is nothing wrong with helping our family but, there are some family members that the more you help them, the more help they want. As you continue to bail them out, they continue to do their thing at your expense.

They continue to choose loser men who beat them, take their money, car, etc. They continue to have babies that they can't take care of. They drop out of school. They can't/won't keep a job. It is not your place to continue to support that. These are hindrances to keep you from doing what you need or want to do, or are destined to do.

**SOMETHING TO THINK ABOUT:**

What obstacles are stopping you from moving forward? Who or what are the hindrances in your life?

# Not Good Enough

Lack of self-esteem will keep you from **"doing it"** When you don't feel like you are goo enough to do something you won't make a move. You might have people in your life who tell you that you are not smart enough, talented enough, pretty enough, thin enough. They may say that you are too old, not old enough. They may say any number of negative things to dissuade you from moving forward. You may be telling yourself these same things. These are self-defeating thoughts and you must STOP IT!

Your self-talk may be very negative. Words take on meaning. After saying it and hearing it for so long you soon find yourself believing it. The Bible says as a man thinketh so is he. You soon find yourself unable to imagine yourself doing anything grand. You become content with your little bit, your mediocre life. You push aside your dream to own your own business, travel the world, write a book.

Women, sometimes the man in your life is the one filling our heads with the negativity. I have had several friends who had men who were less than supportive. Sometimes they were very critical of them, often in front of others. It would aggravate me so much. I would be so angry seeing these beautiful, talented, women being mistreated and disrespected by these losers.

Sometimes because we fear being alone, we take being mistreated. We allow men to dictate to us, to hold us back, to keep us from **"doing it"** Some men don't want their women to outshine them. As long as they are the big dog, then it's all good. If you have a man who wants to hold you back...Let him go! You want a man who will support all of your dreams.

Men, you also need to have a woman who supports the things you want to do. I know a few men who are not getting the support they need from their woman, but they hang in there because they don't want to be alone. Just like I told my sisters, you want a woman in your life to support all of your dreams. Men and women, remove from your life anybody who keeps you from following your dreams

I am so blessed to have a husband who is very supportive. He sees in me thing that I don't see. He once told me that I should apply for a position dealing with lots of numbers, spreadsheets and big budgets. He got impatient when I told him I was not qualified and started giving him the reasons why I felt I was not qualified.

At the time I could not even do a simple excel spreadsheet and everybody who knows me knows that math is not my friend. His exact words to me were "Then say you don't want the job, not that you can't do it. You can do anything you choose to do" My husband believes that I can do anything I choose to do. Every woman needs that kind of support in her life.

**SOMETHING TO THINK ABOUT:**

In what areas of your life do you think you are not good enough? What are you going to do about it?

# My Tongue

The tongue is a small instrument with a whole lot of power. The Bible says that there is life and death in the power of the tongue. We must be careful that we are not killing our dreams with our words. We must be careful of the words we speak about our lives. We should not speak negatively about what we want to get accomplished in our lives.

We need to speak positively. Words have a life of their own. We need to be careful of our thoughts. Remember our thoughts become words which then become our actions. The moment you speak something out loud you give birth to it.

If there is something you want to do, or feel you should be doing, you need to begin declaring it out loud. Say it. Tell other people. This will hold you accountable. Remember, you don't want to tell the naysayers who are going to laugh at your or try to change your mind. You want to tell people who support you, who support your dreams, and who will hold you accountable.

When you speak out loud your plans you put the ball in motion. When I decided to write this book I spoke it out loud. Then I told people. There is something about putting it out there that will move you to action. I told people because then I could not fall into my old habit of procrastination. I knew these people would keep me on my toes. They were going to hold me accountable. If I said I was writing a book then they would be looking for a book.

Words have power. We know that in the natural, words spoken out loud have the power to hurt someone's feelings or to encourage someone who is feeling down. Words are just as powerful in the spiritual realm. Some positive words can change your life and allow you to get in line with God's will for your life.

Positive affirmations are declarations of truth. Webster's Dictionary says that when you affirm something you declare positively, you make firm. When you speak positive things about yourself it motivates you. When you get in the habit of speaking positively about yourself your life will begin to change.

Thoughts are real, and our thoughts and words create our reality. I will say this again. It is just that important…Be careful with the words you use to talk about yourself. Your words could be what is stopping you from doing all the things you want to do the most.

So go ahead and speak life to whatever it is you want to do. Speak it, write it, talk about it. Don't dwell on the things that you can't do, or the reasons why it won't work. Don't wait until…until never comes. Do it now. Do it old, do it young, do it fat, do thin. Just do it now. And then declare it loud and clear. **"I'm Doing It!"**

**Even so the tongue is a little member, and boasteth great things. Behold how great a matter a little fire kindleth! James 3:5 (KJV)**

**Likewise, the tongue is a small part of the body, but it makes great boasts. Consider what a great forest is on fire by a small spark. James 3:5 (NIV)**

**But the tongue can no mane tame; it is an unruly, evil, full of deadly poison. James 3:5 (KJV)**

**But no mane can tame the tongue. It is a restless evil full of deadly poison. James 3:8 (NIV)**

**SOMETHING TO THINK ABOUT:**

What words do you use to talk about you?

# The End

When God puts something in your heart to do…**Do it!** When you don't pursue the thing you want to do, you become passive about it. It becomes easy to put it off. Quit making excuses. Get focused. Stop putting things off.

Every morning get into the habit of commanding your day. Look in the mirror and declare "today I am going to…" "today I am…" "today I will…" You finish the sentences. What is it you want to do? See yourself doing whatever it is.

Remember tomorrow never comes. You have to stop planning to do something and just do it. Quit being passive and start pursuing your dreams today. Make up your mind and say "Today I am **doing it!** Whatever **"it"** is

Don't miss your opportunity. Remember there is a season and a time for everything. Is it your time? Don't miss your season.

How many great ideas do you have but you're waiting to get started on executing them? Start today, right where you are. Go from planning to do, to **Doing It!**

*Don't wait for tomorrow*

*For tomorrow never comes*

*If there are things you want to do*

*Then quickly get them done*

*Don't look back over your life*

*And think about what could have been*

*For that is just as awful waste of time to spend*

*There is nothing wrong with failing*

*And having to start again*

*It is only wrong if you never begin*

~~~~~~~~~~~~~

*Conchetta Jones*

## About the Author

Conchetta Jones lives in Chicago, IL. She has a Bachelor of Arts Degree in Interdisciplinary Studies and a Masters in Communication and Training from Governors State University. Conchetta works for the Girl Scouts of Greater Chicago and Northwest Indiana as a Community Engagement Manager. She loves the work that she does mentoring girls both on the job and in her personal life. Conchetta volunteers for several organizations but one that holds a special place in her heart is the American Cancer Society. She works with the Relay for Life Campaign in memory of her brother Wille.